Plants

Flowers

Patricia Whitehouse

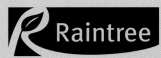

Raintree

www.raintreepublishers.co.uk
Visit our website to find out more information about **Raintree** books.

To order:
☎ Phone 44 (0) 1865 888112
▤ Send a fax to 44 (0) 1865 314091
🖥 Visit the Raintree Bookshop at **www.raintreepublishers.co.uk** to browse our catalogue and order online.

First published in Great Britain by Raintree,
Halley Court, Jordan Hill, Oxford OX2 8EJ,
part of Harcourt Education.
Raintree is a registered trademark of Harcourt
Education Ltd.

Editorial: Nick Hunter and Diyan Leake
Design: Sue Emerson (HL-US) and Joanna Sapwell
(www.tipani.co.uk)
Picture Research: Amor Montes de Oca (HL-US)
Production: Jonathan Smith

Originated by Dot Gradations
Printed and bound in China by South China
Printing Company

ISBN 1 844 21064 2

British Library Cataloguing in Publication Data
Whitehouse, Patricia
Flowers
575.6
A full catalogue record for this book is available
from the British Library.

Acknowledgements
The publishers would like to thank the following
for permission to reproduce photographs:
Bruce Coleman Inc. pp. **12L** (Jane Burton), **17** (Joy
Spurr); Color Pic, Inc. pp. **1**, **14** (E. R. Degginger),
23 (petal, E. R. Degginger), back cover (petals, E. R.
Degginger); Corbis pp. **9** (Peter Smithers), **23** (bud,
Peter Smithers); David Derr pp. **7**, **22**, **23** (pistil),
24; Dwight Kuhn pp. **5**, **18**; Ed Reschke p. **13R**; Jay
Ireland & Georgienne E. Bradley/Bradleyireland.com
p. **10**; McDonald Wildlife Photography pp. **20** (Joe
McDonald), **23** (nectar, Joe McDonald); Nancy
Rotenberg pp. **4**, **8**, **13L**, **23** (stem); National
Geographic Society p. **11** (Michael Nichols); Rick
Wetherbee p. **19**; Sally Beyer pp. **6** (Greg Ryan), **23**
(pollen, Greg Ryan; stamen, Greg Ryan), back cover
(pollen, Greg Ryan); Visuals Unlimited pp. **12R**
(Arthur R. Hill), **15** (Cheryl Hogue); Winston Fraser
p. **16**.

Cover photograph of sunflowers reproduced with
permission of Nancy Rotenberg

Every effort has been made to contact copyright
holders of any material reproduced in this book.
Any omissions will be rectified in subsequent
printings if notice is given to the publishers.

Some words are shown in bold, **like this.** You can find them in the glossary on page 23.

Contents

What are flowers?

stem

Flowers are a part of some plants.

They grow on the ends of **branches** or **stems**.

Flowers grow on trees, too.

These are the flowers on an oak tree.

Why do plants have flowers?

pollen

stamen

Flowers make seeds.

First, a yellow dust called **pollen** forms on the **stamens** in a flower.

pistil

Next, the pollen drops into the **pistil**.

Then seeds start to grow.

What are flower buds?

Buds are flowers that have not opened yet.

They need sunlight to open them up.

petals

bud

When a bud opens, you can see the flower and its colourful **petals**.

How big are flowers?

orchid

Flowers come in many sizes.

The orchid in this picture is tiny.

Some flowers are very big.

This is the biggest flower in
the world.

How many flowers can plants have?

Some plants have one flower.

Some have more.

A sunflower looks like one big flower, but it's not.

Each yellow part in the middle is one tiny flower!

What do flowers look like?

Flowers come in many shapes.

Some flowers have lots of petals.

Some flowers have only a few petals.

These flowers look like birds.

What do flowers smell like?

Different flowers have different smells.

Many flowers smell nice.

These flowers smell horrible!

They are called skunk cabbage.

How do people use flowers?

People use some flowers for food.

When you eat broccoli, you are eating flowers.

People use some flowers to make perfume.

People give flowers as presents.

How do animals use flowers?

Birds and insects use flowers for food.

They drink a juice called **nectar** from the flower.

Some insects and spiders hide inside flowers.

They can hide there because their colour matches the flower.

Quiz

What parts of this flower do you remember?

Look for the answers on page 24.

Glossary

bud
flower or leaf that is still tightly closed

nectar
sweet juice in flowers

petal
coloured or white outer part of a flower

pistil
the part of a flower that makes seeds

pollen
yellow dust in flowers

stamen
the part of a flower that makes pollen

stem
the part of a plant where the buds, leaves and flowers grow

Index

Answers to quiz on page 22

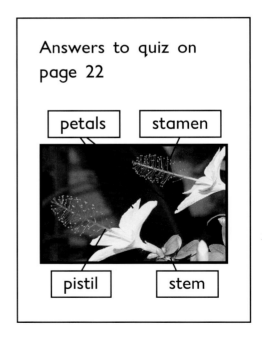

petals   stamen

pistil   stem

24

Titles in the Plants series include:

Hardback   1 844 21064 2

Hardback   1 844 21065 0

Hardback   1 844 21066 9

Hardback   1 844 21067 7

Hardback   1 844 21068 5

Hardback   1 844 21069 3

Find out about the other titles in this series on our website www.raintreepublishers.co.uk